Embracing the Author Within

A New Approach to Life & Publishing for Leaders

Gina Gardiner

Embracing the Author Within – A New Approach to Life & Publishing for Leaders

Copyright © 2020 by Georgina Gardiner

All rights reserved: No part of this publication may be reproduced, distributed or transmitted in any form or by any means, including photocopying, recording, or other electronic or mechanical methods, without the prior written permission of the publisher, except in the case of brief quotations embodied in critical reviews and certain other non-commercial uses permitted by copyright law. For permission requests, write to the publisher, addressed "Attention: Permissions Coordinator", at the email address below.

Limit of Liability: The information contained in this book is for information purposes only and may not apply to your situation. The author, publisher, distributor, and provider supply no warranty about the content or accuracy of content enclosed. Information provided is subjective. Keep this in mind when reviewing this guide. Although the author and publisher have made every eff ort to ensure that the information in this book was correct at press time, the author and publisher do not assume and hereby disclaim any liability to any party for any loss, damage, or disruption caused by errors or omissions, whether such errors or omissions result from negligence, accident, or any other cause.

Disclaimer: The information provided by Gina or any guests are not intended to diagnose or prescribe medical or psychological conditions nor to claim to prevent, treat, mitigate or to cure such conditions. The information contained is not intended to replace a one-on one relationship with a doctor or mental health professional. All examples in this book are just that—examples. They are not intended to represent or guarantee that everyone will achieve the same results. You understand that each individual's success will be determined by their desire, dedication, background, effort, and motivation to work.

"The typical result one can expect to achieve is nothing". The "typical" person never gets to the end of this book. The "typical" person fails to implement anything. Thus, they change nothing. Zero. That's because "typical" people do nothing, and therefore, they achieve nothing. Be atypical. Do something. Implement something. If it doesn't work, make a change, and implement that. Try again. Try harder. Persist. And reap the rewards.

Contact Gina:
LinkedIn: linkedin.com/in/ginagardinerassociates
Facebook: facebook.com/genuinelyyouprograms
Facebook Group: facebook.com/groups/genuinelyyou

Websites:
genuinely-you.com
enlightenedleadership.co
gina.gardiner.com

Email: gina@genuinely-you.com
Tumblr: tumblr.com/blog/enlightenedleadersuccessvault
Please subscribe to the 'Genuinely You with Gina Gardiner' YouTube channel.

DEDICATION

Once again, I would like to thank all the many people who have helped and supported me on my journey. I am truly grateful for your wisdom, encouragement, and the lessons you have taught me along the way.

ACKNOWLEDGMENTS

As always, I am so grateful for the help of my assistant Rachel Davidson – a truly talented novelist. Her ongoing support means so much to me. Thank you!
Rachel has contributed to this book, offering you the benefit of her expertise and knowledge of self-publishing to help you navigate the process. Details of her amazing three-book 'Beyond Veils' Series is at the back of the book – A trilogy of spiritual novels, they are well worth the read!

A huge thank you to the amazing AliNICOLE WOW! – the 'Ultimate Industry Disruptor' who has been my mentor and without whom this book would never have been written. You continue to be a great source of inspiration. I really appreciate your ongoing advice and support.

CONTENTS

Embracing the Author Within a new approach to life & publishing for leaders 3

   A New Approach to Life and to Publishing – My Journey . 3

      Tips on formatting a manuscript ready for upload to Amazon KDP 19

      MOVING FORWARD 22

   Action Planner 23

      MY BOOK - MY BUSINESS - MY PROFITS 83

   OPTIONS FOR SUCCESS 96

   ABOUT THE AUTHOR 103

EMBRACING THE AUTHOR WITHIN A NEW APPROACH TO LIFE & PUBLISHING FOR LEADERS

Time is of the essence!

It is time to be in the moment and seize the opportunity to make the most of your experience and expertise to enhance your credibility, create greater awareness of what you have to offer and to make a positive difference to others. Rip up the rule book you have in your head – instead tune into the experience and expertise you have garnered over the years and to your inner wisdom which is available when you get out of your own way. Use those insights to help you to plan the work and then consistently work the plan. It is a proven route to ongoing success.

A New Approach to Life and to Publishing – My Journey

I published my first books in 2006 and I'm still writing. My publishing journey has been an interesting one - I'd like to share it with you as becoming an author has, I believe, the capacity to set you and your business onto a different trajectory. I hope it will inspire you to start writing if you haven't yet begun or to think very differently about how you can harness the power of publishing to accelerate and support ongoing profitable success if you are already published. My approach to publishing has changed significantly, particularly in recent times.

As an Entrepreneur or business owner becoming a published author has the power to expand your opportunities. I know from personal experience that being a published author can open doors which would have hitherto been closed.

For years, my writing had been limited to writing reports, letters and brochures to be used internally within the school or with parents, the wider community or the authorities. I didn't ever think I would become an author. It simply wasn't on the agenda.

In 2004, I left the world of education where I'd been a Headteacher (Principle) for nearly 21 years because of my health. I had years of experience in developing leadership not only in my own organisation but as the Head of a 'Beacon' school helping many others schools and hundreds of teachers to embrace the principles which underpinned the significant success of my own school, we had been identified on Her Majesties Inspectors Annual 'Best 100 Schools' in England list not once but twice during my tenure. During my time as Head Teacher (Principle) I had also worked for the National College of School Leadership and The London Institute as a trainer-facilitator and for the Government as a Workforce Reform Advisor. I was seen as an expert in my field. However, I was unknown and had little credibility in the business world.

When I left the world of education I realised I wasn't ready for a life of day-time television. I had years of useful experience and expertise and it seemed wrong to waste it.

So, what should I do?

I decided to set up my own business so I could not only use my experience and expertise but choose how, when and where I wanted to work. However, there was a huge shadow between my dream and the reality. Whilst my school was like a business (in the UK schools run their own budget - ours was in excess of one and a half million pounds a year, I employed nearly a hundred staff and was entirely responsible for the fabric of the building ad everything which went on). Ensuring the school was attracting pupils, supporting parents and community, responding to the plethora of government requirements and maintaining standards were just some of our core activities. In reality the school was a business, the profits were well balanced and educated children.

In order to work in the corporate world, I needed a way to demonstrate my level of experience and expertise - and how these were transferable. I realised that simply rocking up and saying, "I'm here," was unlikely to prove to be a successful approach.

I decided to create a research project across a wide range of industries to look at the issues they faced in successfully developing leaders of excellence. I found no matter what the industry was: finance, local government, manufacturing, retail, health, hospitality, insurance, etc. they faced exactly the same challenges around developing excellence in leadership as we had in education. The widgets may be different but people are people.

I now had the confidence that my experience and expertise would be entirely in line with what organisations needed,f HOWEVER I had to find a way of proving it to the decision makers.

I thought carefully about how I could prove my credibility and decided to write two partner books. The first - "Kick Start Your Career," was designed for those who were entering the world of work for the first time. The book offers the reader a short cut to help people transition easily from being at school, college or university into the professional world of work. It is also helpful for those returning to work after a long break. It shares how to become a professional 'grown up' quickly. I based it on my experience of training graduate teachers and probationers to become teachers, something I had been doing for several years.

The second partner book - "Manage Your Staff More Effectively" was designed to do exactly what the title suggests - to help managers get the best out of their teams. It was based on my considerable experience of supporting the development of leadership from emerging leadership to senior management. This is something I had done successfully not only in my own organisation but in many others through our Beacon work and as an Advisor on the Government 'Workforce Reform' project. Through my writing I was able to share over 20 years of practical know-how. I stripped out the industry specific language and concentrated on the principles and strategies which had underpinned the success.

Both books share the principles and strategies I'd developed in my own organisation and with the many others I'd worked with. They are jargon free and will work in pretty well any industry context.

I believe there is a significant difference in writing about what you know and creative writing. Coming from what you know, sharing what has worked in your own context and offering your experience to others is a question of sharing not only your experiences, what has worked and often as useful, what hasn't. It is designed to provide a short cut and a support to others to help them succeed more quickly and easily as they can model their approach on something which has already been shown to work. It is the difference between trying to find your way to somewhere you haven't been before with no map and having a helpful navigational tool. Of course, the reader must put the guidance into context and choose mindfully what is appropriate for them but having the benefit of someone sharing their experience can facilitate a smoother, more efficient journey for others.

As I started the research project, I contacted several established publishing houses. I was thrilled to find a publisher who was interested in what I wanted to write about. HOWEVER, I was told that even with a following wind, the book would not be published for around 18 months. I couldn't wait that long. They also wanted to take control of how the book was to be written and to some extent they wanted to shape the information. In reality the end product would have been very different to that which I intended. I decided to self-publish.

Times were very different in 2005. I had never published before and I was very green. I decided to pay professionals to edit, proof read, design the cover and to set the pages etc. so I could concentrate on the writing. The time scale was much shorter than it would have been had I decided to sign up with the conventional publishing house. Even so - once the book was written it took around 7 months to get the book to print. In those days there were no e-books or print on demand. I paid for each freelance professional and the minimum size print run was 500 books. It cost in excess of £5,000 to have the physical books ready to go.

Both books became very successful calling cards. I was able to send copies to the decision makers within corporates and businesses. This approach resulted in my being booked as a Transformational Leadership Trainer, facilitator and coach on a regular basis with lots of repeat business. The books opened the door for me to talk to the decision makers - once the door was open it was entirely up to me to prove my worth if I wanted to be invited back.

For several years my first two books were a major part of my marketing strategy. After an initial contact by email I would follow up by sending the decision maker within the company a copy of either or both books depending on the circumstances. All went well until the recession in 2008/9. At the start of January 2009, I had contracts in place which would serve me for pretty much the whole year. By mid-

January every contract had been cancelled. Organisations were cancelling their training and development budget. I have always helped individuals and couples through life coaching but it was the leadership training and coaching which was the major earning part of my business. In one week, it was decimated.

I had to re-invent yet again.

My books helped me secure a position as a visiting lecturer at Essex University Business School. One of the benefits of this was that they would also commission me to go and work with companies to provide training or consultancy. Out of this I created a different style of business which I still do to this day. I work on a retainer with businesses helping them through the development of Enlightened Leadership. All of the businesses I have worked with for over 9 months have had significantly positive outcomes: better relationships, less conflict and stress, better wellbeing and work life balance for all, greater productivity and far greater profitability.

2009 was a pivotal year for me. I have been a wheelchair user since 1987 and for many years was completely wheelchair bound. I was talking with Patty, my own coach (I always practice what I preach - you don't have to have a problem to find working a great coach helpful. Offering a sounding board, a support and at times a challenge can bring the best out in you and help you achieve far greater things than you would on your own) Patty asked me why I didn't speak of my disability - she called it 'The elephant in the room' and challenged me to write a book about my story.

Initially I resisted, but after a great deal of thought I made the decision to share my story - I've learned to walk twice as an adult following a serous ski accident and two failed back surgeries and ran my award-winning school for the most part from a wheelchair. Whilst a significant challenge, my disability has actually been a gift. It was hugely instrumental in the creation of my unique approach to helping people step into their true power and the development of Enlightened Leadership. These principles have underpinned the success of my own school and others, and helped the many organisations I've worked with over the years achieve great success too. It is the bedrock of my life's work with individuals, teams and organisations.

The book - "Chariots on Fire" shares some of my story and the principles I used to give myself and the people I worked with, the positive advantage. In reality the published version was the third iteration which took me a couple of years and was a labour of love.

I'd like to share with you the sequence of writing and how writing the book had a profound impact on how I felt about me and life in general.

Version 1: Written as a diary of events with a few strategies at the back for good measure. It was a blow by blow account of my experiences and when I'd finally finished it and read it from front to back I realised that whilst the writing has been cathartic for me, it was of no help what so ever to the reader. I shared it with nobody!

Version 2: I went through the initial draft with a highlight pen and highlighted anything which would be of value to the reader. Rather than it being a diary of events it became a mixture of my story, a much-abridged version but one which still shared the major events AND the strategies and approaches I had used to help me manage the life-changing challenges which had resulted from the accident. I shared this with a professional editor who made some really valuable advice and suggestions about the structure of the book, which bits needed clarification and where I had repeated myself.

Version 3: I used the information from the editor to refine the book and at times to re-write certain sections.

Then, one Sunday morning I was at my computer working on 'Chariots on Fire' when the phone went. It was my sister letting me know that she had just received the dreadful news that our younger brother had suddenly collapsed and died at the side of the road. We were devastated.

When I finally got back to working on the book it felt important that the learning I took from David's death needed to be shared and so the end of the book was re-written.

I share this with you as I have worked with clients who want to write a book but procrastinate because they think it has to be 'perfect' from the outset. As you can see from my experience you simply have to make a start and allow the book to emerge.

I think one of the most important lessons I can share with you is the need to know your WHY? before you start. What is it you want the reader to gain, learn, understand etc. from reading your book? When that is your starting point it becomes so much easier to reverse engineer what you want to say.

'Chariots on Fire,' has since been republished with additions but more of that later.

On this occasion I decided to use an independent company, a sort of 'half way house' to publish my book. It was far quicker and less expensive than my first foray into publishing. The publisher was extremely helpful but I discovered later that their approach to categorising the book was not as effective as it might have been. This had a significant impact on sales. In return for publishing the book they received over half the royalties.

In the early days of Gina Gardiner Associates, 'Kick Start Your Career' and 'Manage Your Staff More Effectively' were a major element in my marketing process however in later years all my clients came to work with me because of recommendations from existing and past clients and by word of mouth. I had plenty of work and did no direct sales or marketing. I would give new clients a copy of the books if it was appropriate but they were no longer the deciding factor in the initial decision to work with me.

'Live Well Eat Well with Coeliac Disease' is a book I put together for a different reason and in a different way. In 1987 I was diagnosed with Coeliac Disease. At that time, I knew nothing about the disease and how to manage it effectively. It is an immune disease which can be controlled effectively by sticking STRICTLY to an entirely gluten free diet. Even a tiny amount of gluten can have a significant impact and every ingestion is thought to increase your chances of developing bowel cancer.

When I was diagnosed the only gluten free bread you could access was on prescription. Very few restaurants know about the problem and thought I was being fussy or faddy. There was very little information available in one place and dealing with the diet was challenging, particularly as my favourite food is cake!

I started to gather information on my condition. Over the years I'd became knowledgeable about which foods were safe or not and had created template letters to use with restaurants and hotels to make life easier when I was away from home. I recognised how important mindset and approach are in dealing with any condition which impacts on your life. Eating out at friends' houses or restaurants had to be managed carefully and it would have been easy to let managing the disease run my life.

More and more often I was being approached by people who had been recently diagnosed or their family members and I was constantly repeating the same information. In 2017 I decided to collate the information and write it in book form. It was a case of collating the information I'd gathered in a coherent way. Once again, I used the same indepenedent publisher as I had for the first version of 'Chariots on Fire'.

By late 2017 I was becoming increasingly concerned about the growing number of people who were stressed or anxious and lacking in confidence and the increasing number of businesses which were struggling because of poor leadership. I was working with more and more life coaching clients who were really struggling because they were on the receiving end of poor leadership or people who had been promoted and were struggling to manage their role because of the lack of adequate training. The news was full of examples of poor leadership, and its impact. This included the growing numbers of people on anti-depressants and of people struggling with stress, anxiety and depression because of work.

I had a growing sense of purpose and a drive to make a make a positive difference to more people. I knew how profound and positive a difference the approach to leadership I had developed and shared with a wide variety of businesses could make but I needed to find an effective way to share it. I decided to set up a second business, Genuinely You Ltd. I wanted to find a way to reach out to people on a far bigger scale. Using the Internet was the perfect vehicle.

I realised I would need to do things very differently. I had done no marketing at all for many years. At this time, I had a very limited internet presence. I had a Face Book page and a LinkedIn account but rarely used either. I had a tiny data base and so there was a real need to find an effective way of building meaningful contacts quickly. My coach at the time suggested that I offer a free PDF download of "Chariots on Fire" as a lead magnet so I could build my data base quickly. Great idea BUT—the publisher would not allow me to use the book in this way. I felt frustrated by the lack of control - it was time for a re-think!!

John, my coach, recommended that I republish "Chariots on Fire" with a range of case studies. He offers a publishing service where I could retain complete editorial control. I decided to re-purpose the book and added new information and some case studies. My coach has great experience in helping authors achieve No 1 International Best Seller Status, he understands how best to use the categorisation for example and as a result helped me get my first best seller. I was thrilled!!

By May 2017 I realised it was time to write another book. My thinking had moved on, I'd up-levelled since writing "Chariots on Fire" in 2009 and I had several year's more experience of working with individual clients and strategically with leaders and businesses to draw upon.

I spent that summer frantically writing in every spare moment, often late into the night. By September it was done - over 70,000 words. I handed the draft over to John and the publishing arm of his business dealt with all the technical stuff. As a result, "Thriving Not Surviving - The 5 Secret Pathways to Happiness, Success and Fulfilment" was published in late September.

I also created a companion journal to support people who wanted to embrace the approach shared in the book. The book was offered as a lead generator in PDF form through Linked In and Facebook. The main intentions of the campaign were to increase the visibility and credibility of the business and to increase the size of the data base. It achieved both. It became my second No 1 International Best seller.

The book is designed to be at the heart of the Personal and Spiritual programme I created to help people step into their genuine power - to become the 'Leader in Their Own Life'. I also created a themed journal for the course and published a version of "Thriving Not Surviving" with a 30-day journal.

For each of the books I had approached writing in a very specific way. In the first instance I was very clear about why I was writing the book and what I wanted the reader to get out of reading it BEFORE I started writing anything. I then plotted out each of the elements which would be needed to achieve the goal. I created an over-all plan with chapter headings and sub sections. Once the plan was created it allowed me to write the book out of sequence depending on what I was drawn to write and the amount of time available.

Once each section was completed, I put it together, read it, re-ordered it, re-read it and ensured there was a flow from start to finish.

My next book, the "7 Day Happiness Challenge" was created in a very different way. I ran a 7-day Facebook Happiness Challenge Video series as part of my strategic plan to help people, to share my approach, build my brand and to become better known on social media.

Each day I did a Facebook Live video sharing a range of strategies and principles to help people feel happier more easily and more consistently. Each of the strategies I included had been proven to work not only for myself but also for the countless clients I'd shared them with. Once they were completed the videos were transcribed and edited and became the core of a book called "The 7 Day Happiness Challenge." Creating a book in this way was a far easier and less time-consuming process than any I had used previously.

This approach won't work for everyone but is a useful one to think about, particularly if you enjoy speaking. For those of you who are nervous of writing, you may find using this approach or one of the many different pieces of technology which record and transcribe simultaneously helpful. It is a great way to get started. However, it is important to speak clearly to get the best out of the technology. If you have an accent you will need to experiment as software differs enormously in the level of accuracy and tolerance to pronunciation and tonality.

Be aware that you will need to edit your transcript very carefully. I've found some great bloopers in the transcripts where the software has mis-interpreted what I had said. You will find that the structure of sentences often changes when you speak and may need attention. You will certainly discover all the idiosyncrasies in the way you speak, how you give yourself thinking time by saying 'erm' etc. and any habitual patterns of language you use.

Editing and proof reading gives you a great opportunity to decide if you have captured the real essence of what you wanted to share. It is a good idea to edit several times and to get someone else to read and give feedback as it is incredibly easy to miss things. As the writer you are too close to your writing. I know from personal experience that often I've missed really obvious things as I've read what I meant to say rather than what I actually wrote.

Many people believe that you have to do everything alone and that may feel true. However, contributing a chapter to other people's publications can be a good way to get started. The reality is that collaboration can be a great way to create a book quickly and easily by sharing the load. The creative act of brain storming can spark off lots of ideas. I was involved as a contributor to 'The Change Series' and have collaborated on other projects since then. The series was coordinated by the organisers who created the central theme and each person wrote a chapter. The organisers arranged for the editing, proof reading and publishing of the book. Creating a chapter around the theme of the book requires far less commitment in terms of time and effort whilst giving you the exposure and credibility of being an author.

Until this point the approach to writing a book had been fairly similar but things were about to change. I met AliNICOLE WOW who has since become my mentor. She introduced me to a whole new approach to profitable publishing.

The next phase of my publishing journey had begun.

Through my work with AliNICOLE WOW I have begun writing a very different style of book.

Her advice is to keep it simple and to create workbooks or intentional journals, and to create a stable of publications with a wide selection of offerings which showcase your experience and expertise. Doing so greatly increases your profitability.

This book is a perfect example. In it I am sharing my experience which is intended to give you the reader food for thought, a sense of possibility and to inspire action in a very specific way. The questions at the back which form the workbook or intentional journal are designed to help you identify potential themes you could write about and some strategies to help you get going.

It is all too easy to dismiss the wealth of knowledge and insights you have developed over the years. To you it may feel 'It's just what I do,' however what you dismiss as 'just' can very often can help others to learn, avoid making costly mistakes and to move forward more quickly.

If you are unfamiliar with writing it can be really helpful to start blogging or writing articles. If you get organised and plan effectively you can create your publication - blog by blog or article by article. It feels so much less overwhelming if you tackle things in bite size pieces. You wouldn't eat a whole cow or an entire field of corn in one sitting, you'd get terrible indigestion! You can build your book from the completed blogs and articles if that approach suits you. You may find it easier if you create an over-arching structure where each article or blog is a chapter or a subsection.

As I've already said, if you feel more confident speaking rather than writing you can use technology to help you with the bulk of the writing. I'm currently experimenting with speaking into software which transcribes speech. It works well when I'm really clear about what I want to say but I recognise that I often organise my thoughts through the act of writing. There is no 'right' or 'wrong way,' you need to find your own way. I have leant to experiment and have often been surprised to discover how varying the approach can make a significant difference, so please be open minded.

Being intentional about what you want to achieve and WHY? is really important. When you have clarity of intention it not only helps at a very practical level as your efforts become so much more focused and efficient, but it also creates the best platform for your interaction with your inner wisdom and universal consciousness. This is one of the underpinning principles of profitable publishing.

Becoming a published author doesn't need to be difficult. Times have changed and made it incredibly easy to self-publish. The reality is that if you have an Amazon Account you can publish at zero cost if you are prepared to learn how to use the KDP Amazon Publisher software. You can even design the cover using an image from their bank of images or import your own.

For those of you who find technology intimidating it is something you can employ someone else to do. However, like all things if you are prepared to invest time in learning how to do it - it will get easier with subsequent publications. I like to send for a draft copy to do a final check before the book is submitted for publication so I can see the book in the flesh and do a final proof read. Once completed it is a simple step to publish the book for real. A few days later the book goes live and you are then a published author!

Writing a work of fiction comes from a different stable, as my good friend and assistant Rachel Davidson, a spiritual novelist will attest to. Tapping into your creativity and writing a novel (or in her case a trilogy) requires a very different approach. I am in awe of her capacity to write hugely engaging stories which make me think about life in a different way, and both laugh and cry in equal measure. You will find her details of her books at the end of this book; I can thoroughly recommend them!

It is Rachel who takes my writing and does all the formatting for me. To help you, Rachel has put together some tips and strategies to help you navigate the process of taking your script and publishing it. Rachel has not only published her own trilogy of novels under the series title of 'Beyond Veils' (a great read!) she has done the admin work to publish several of my books on Amazon KDP.

This approach allows you to stay in the driving seat and for the timescale to be in your control.

So, why write a book?

Books are:

- A great way to provide information and support to many people
- A basis for key note speeches
- A route to access guest appearances in the media
- Can be used as the core of a Media Tour
- A great way to offer you exposure to a wider audience
- The conduit to the reader engaging in activities which offer far higher levels of profitability - VIP Intensives, Courses, Seminars, Retreats, Media Tours, other goods and services
- Having multiple streams of potential profitability within your business is important and will become even more important as we move forward into the new era.
- Becoming an author of multiple books is an important way of supporting your profitability.

Of course, writing a book requires an investment - that investment is your time but I think that time is well spent. Being a published author gives you credibility in your chosen field. I have been offered many opportunities to speak, to contribute to other publications, appear as a guest on podcasts, radio and TV as a result of being a published author.

I think it is important to plan what you want the book to achieve before you write it. Consider in your planning that there may be more than one purpose to your book. Writing multiple books based on an overall strategic business plan has the potential to catapult your business to a whole new level. Identifying the products and services connected to the books in a focused and intentional way creates a very powerful expansion energy which offers significant opportunities for success.

Tips on formatting a manuscript ready for upload to Amazon KDP

Decide early on in your publishing process what "trim size" you want your paperback book to be. This is the size of your book and once your book is published this cannot be changed. You might not think this is a problem, but make sure you are sure, because if for any reason the size of your paperback does become a problem (perhaps your local book store will only stock books of a particular size because of their shelving configuration) you cannot easily solve this.

Assuming that you're using a PC and are writing your manuscript in Word (MAC users have access to more refined publishing tools such as Vellum, that has richer book formatting functionality) - download the set of Amazon trim-size templates which KDP makes available.

Once you have your pre-formatted template you can choose to either copy and paste your original manuscript into this pre-formatted template, or simply type your manuscript straight into the template (if you are really organised and thought about formatting before you thought of starting your book!). These pre-formatted templates are a fantastic tool having the required page margins and page mirroring already set up. They also have the different 'sections' within MS Word created - enabling your book to have certain pages to have page numbers and others to not have them (a simple concept, but surprisingly tricky to successfully set-up in MS Word). Within your Amazon KDP log-in, there is the option for "KDP Help Centre" - click on this and search using keywords related to manuscript trim-size templates.

Make sure that when you come to copy and paste your manuscript into the pre-formatted trim-size template you are absolutely sure your manuscript is edited and proof-read. Ideally, you do not want to be 'messing about' with the formatted manuscript version as in doing so you risk upsetting the pre-set formatting. Much better to be dealing with the absolute final manuscript, to minimise how much editing you need to do in the formatted template document.

You've probably written your manuscript in a default font that makes sense for you as you work through your ideas, maybe arial, maybe times new roman - but this doesn't necessarily make your final book look the best it can be. Amazon's default templates have pre-set fonts for "body text" in each chapter, as well as chapter headings, sub-headings etc. As you go through copying and pasting text from one document to the other, it is a good habit to use the "Paste Special > Unformatted Text" option within MS Word. This ensures that the incoming text and its formatting doesn't disrupt the pre-set formatting in the Amazon template.

Remember that KDP has certain rules pertaining to manuscripts - for instance, you must not have too many blank pages (as this can end up looking like a printing mistake and that means Amazon will get returns and complaints - hassle for them to deal with and not their fault if you've published the book with blank pages).

Most criteria that Amazon will object to can be researched within the KDP Help Centre before uploading your manuscript to KDP. Be aware however, that Amazon KDP will do a quality-check on your paperback once you've submitted for publication and, if they find any issues they will refuse publication and email you with details of why.

When your manuscript is uploaded into Amazon KDP you will be able to preview what the paperback looks like. Do this! You may find that, even though you have used an Amazon Template, there will be anomalies once the manuscript is within KDP's systems. Things like certain content not appearing on the right-hand page as is normally the book publishing convention or having "orphaned" sentences - a single line of text upon a page. You'll need to take a note of these, return to your manuscript in MS Word and correct the issues, before reuploading and rechecking the paperback preview.

All of the above applies for the formatting of eBooks too - although the publication guidelines are a little less stringent. For instance, eBooks allow readers to re-size text, so issues such as orphaned sentences do not tend to occur.

Finally, if you need more help then organisations such as the Alliance of Independent Authors have databases of book-publishing services in which you can find professionals capable of assisting you with all areas of book publication. This information is made available to members of the Alliance of Independent Authors - with varying levels of membership are available.

See allianceindependentauthors.org for more details

MOVING FORWARD

The Action Planner/Intentional Journal Section of this book is designed to help you tune into your own inner wisdom and to connect with the power of universal energy. This will help you become more confident as a writer and ultimately help you to achieve success as a published author. Use the questions to help you shape your thoughts.

Journaling is an incredible tool designed to help the writer of the journal achieve their goals and manifest their dreams. Taking the time to be quiet, to listen to the inner voice and to write without filtering or judgement on a regular basis is a game changer. Do not under-estimate its power!

There are also some simple templates at the end of the book to help you in the planning process.

It is important to recognise that the grand gesture does little to help. It is the daily actions consistently taken which will make the difference.

ACTION PLANNER

1) Imagine you have your published book in your hand. How does it feel?

The more you engage with the emotions this will generate the better. Who would you tell? What reaction would you have?

2) The following questions are designed to help you consider potential themes.

Think of your strengths and areas of expertise? Start to create a list, it is one you can add to as things occur to you. Once you have identified your list take each entry in turn.

Focus on one per day and think about the following questions. Don't be limited by my questions they are just a starting point.

Consider your professional/ business life, your personal life – lifestyle, health, hobbies, interests etc.

Today simply do a brainstorm of ideas – at least once a week come back to the list and add any further thoughts and ideas.

Week 1 – Identify the idea – who would it help? Why?

(There is space in the next few pages to record your thoughts. The next activities start on page 35.)

2) Cont'd – Week 2 - Identify the idea – who would it help? Why?

2) Cont'd – Week 3 - Identify the idea – who would it help? Why?

2) Cont'd – Week 4 - Identify the idea – who would it help? Why?

2) Cont'd – Week 5 - Identify the idea – who would it help? Why?

2) Cont'd – Week 6 - Identify the idea – who would it help? Why?

2) Cont'd – Week 7 - Identify the idea – who would it help? Why?

2) Cont'd – Week 8 - Identify the idea – who would it help? Why?

2) Cont'd – Week 9 - Identify the idea – who would it help? Why?

2) Cont'd – Week 10 - Identify the idea – who would it help? Why?

3)   Option 1

Create a short description for one of the areas you identified on your Brain Storm list. Think about how you gained the skill or expertise.

Imagine you were a complete novice.

What information, insights or advice would have helped you to save time, energy, money or aggravation?

What worked well – why was that?

What went wrong – what did you learn – how did/could you have avoided it?

4)   Option 2

Create a short description for one of the areas you identified on your brain storm list. Think about how you gained the skill or expertise.

Imagine you were a complete novice.

What information, insights or advice would have helped you to save time, energy, money or aggravation?

What worked well – why was that?

What went wrong – what did you learn – how did/could you have avoided it?

5)   Option 3

Create a short description for one of the areas you identified on your brain storm list. Think about how you gained the skill or expertise.

Imagine you were a complete novice.

What information, insights or advice would have helped you to save time, energy, money or aggravation?

What worked well – why was that?

What went wrong – what did you learn – how did/could you have avoided it?

6)   Option 4

Create a short description for one of the areas you identified on your brain storm list. Think about how you gained the skill or expertise.

Imagine you were a complete novice.

What information, insights or advice would have helped you to save time, energy, money or aggravation?

What worked well – why was that?

What went wrong – what did you learn – how did/could you have avoided it?

7) Option 5

Create a short description for one of the areas you identified on your brain storm list. Think about how you gained the skill or expertise.

Imagine you were a complete novice.

What information, insights or advice would have helped you to save time, energy, money or aggravation?

What worked well – why was that?

What went wrong – what did you learn – how did/could you have avoided it?

8)   Option 6

Create a short description for one of the areas you identified on your brain storm list. Think about how you gained the skill or expertise.

Imagine you were a complete novice.

What information, insights or advice would have helped you to save time, energy, money or aggravation?

What worked well – why was that?

What went wrong – what did you learn – how did/could you have avoided it?

9) Option 7

Create a short description for one of the areas you identified on your brain storm list. Think about how you gained the skill or expertise.

Imagine you were a complete novice.

What information, insights or advice would have helped you to save time, energy, money or aggravation?

What worked well – why was that?

What went wrong – what did you learn – how did/could you have avoided it?

10)   Option 8

Create a short description for one of the areas you identified on your brain storm list. Think about how you gained the skill or expertise.

Imagine you were a complete novice.

What information, insights or advice would have helped you to save time, energy, money or aggravation?

What worked well – why was that?

What went wrong – what did you learn – how did/could you have avoided it?

11)   Option 9

Create a short description for one of the areas you identified on your brain storm list. Think about how you gained the skill or expertise.

Imagine you were a complete novice.

What information, insights or advice would have helped you to save time, energy, money or aggravation?

What worked well – why was that?

What went wrong – what did you learn – how did/could you have avoided it?

12)   Option 10

Create a short description for one of the areas you identified on your brain storm list. Think about how you gained the skill or expertise.

Imagine you were a complete novice.

What information, insights or advice would have helped you to save time, energy, money or aggravation?

What worked well – why was that?

What went wrong – what did you learn – how did/could you have avoided it?

How you would support and mentor someone else to develop those strengths for themselves. What would you be saying to them?

and/or experience.

13) Think about the experience of identifying your skills and areas of expertise.

How does this make you feel?

How would it feel to help someone else develop and grow in confidence and competence?

14) Think about the challenges you have overcome in your life? Think about health – physical, mental, emotional, spiritual, relationships – personal and professional, growing up, dealing with life challenges – dealing with finding a job, redundancy, money, etc.

What have you learned and how could you use your experience to help others to do the same? Spend some time creating a list. Over the following days take each thing on the list answer the questions. Remember the questions are just a starting point.

15)   Challenge 1

Create a short description for one of the challenges you identified on your brain storm list. Think about the challenge - what led up to it?

What impact did the challenge have on you/your family/your colleagues? Why?

How did you deal with the challenge?

What worked and why?

What didn't work and how did you deal with it?

What was your mindset/attitude?

What advice would you give your youngers self about this challenge if you had the luxury of hindsight?

16) Challenge 2

Create a short description for one of the challenges you identified on your brain storm list. Think about the challenge - what led up to it?

What impact did the challenge have on you/your family/your colleagues? Why?

How did you deal with the challenge?

What worked and why?

What didn't work and how did you deal with it?

What was your mindset/attitude?

What advice would you give your youngers self about this challenge if you had the luxury of hindsight?

17)   Challenge 3

Create a short description for one of the challenges you identified on your brain storm list. Think about the challenge - what led up to it?

What impact did the challenge have on you/your family/your colleagues? Why?

How did you deal with the challenge?

What worked and why?

What didn't work and how did you deal with it?

What was your mindset/attitude?

What advice would you give your youngers self about this challenge if you had the luxury of hindsight?

18)   Challenge 4

Create a short description for one of the challenges you identified on your brain storm list. Think about the challenge - what led up to it?

What impact did the challenge have on you/your family/your colleagues? Why?

How did you deal with the challenge?

What worked and why?

What didn't work and how did you deal with it?

What was your mindset/attitude?

What advice would you give your youngers self about this challenge if you had the luxury of hindsight?

19) Challenge 5

Create a short description for one of the challenges you identified on your brain storm list. Think about the challenge - what led up to it?

What impact did the challenge have on you/your family / your colleagues? Why?

How did you deal with the challenge?

What worked and why?

What didn't work and how did you deal with it?

What was your mindset/attitude?

What advice would you give your youngers self about this challenge if you had the luxury of hindsight?

20)   Challenge 6

Create a short description for one of the challenges you identified on your brain storm list. Think about the challenge - what led up to it?

What impact did the challenge have on you/your family/your colleagues? Why?

How did you deal with the challenge?

What worked and why?

What didn't work and how did you deal with it?

What was your mindset/attitude?

What advice would you give your youngers self about this challenge if you had the luxury of hindsight?

21) Challenge 7

Create a short description for one of the challenges you identified on your brain storm list. Think about the challenge - what led up to it?

What impact did the challenge have on you/your family/your colleagues? Why?

How did you deal with the challenge?

What worked and why?

What didn't work and how did you deal with it?

What was your mindset/attitude?

What advice would you give your youngers self about this challenge if you had the luxury of hindsight?

22) Challenge 8

Create a short description for one of the challenges you identified on your brain storm list. Think about the challenge - what led up to it?

What impact did the challenge have on you/your family/your colleagues? Why?

How did you deal with the challenge?

What worked and why?

What didn't work and how did you deal with it?

What was your mindset/attitude?

What advice would you give your youngers self about this challenge if you had the luxury of hindsight?

23)   Challenge 9

Create a short description for one of the challenges you identified on your brain storm list. Think about the challenge - what led up to it?

What impact did the challenge have on you/your family/your colleagues? Why?

How did you deal with the challenge?

What worked and why?

What didn't work and how did you deal with it?

What was your mindset/attitude?

What advice would you give your youngers self about this challenge if you had the luxury of hindsight?

24)   Challenge 10

Create a short description for one of the challenges you identified on your brain storm list. Think about the challenge - what led up to it?

What impact did the challenge have on you / your family / your colleagues? Why?

How did you deal with the challenge?

What worked and why?

What didn't work and how did you deal with it?

What was your mindset/attitude?

What advice would you give your youngers self about this challenge if you had the luxury of hindsight?

25) What skills, hobbies, interests or passions do you have which others may share which would be of potential interest to others?

You don't have to be a grand master to be of service to others. It is often easier to learn from those who are a few steps ahead of you as they are able to appreciate the challenge of learning. I.T. is a great example, in my experience those who are masters of the computer and software often go too quickly or use language which is too technical.

Other examples of hobbies or interests where your knowledge and experience may be of use to others include cookery, gardening, art, craft, collectables, getting or keeping fit, clock making, calligraphy etc. The list is endless...

26) What insights have you developed in life that have been significant and why?

27) Think about the approaches you have developed in your business which could help others save time, money or resources?

28) What has helped you on your journey to success in life/in business?

Think about the people who have supported/challenged you – what did they say or do? What was the impact?

29) What has helped you on your journey to success in life/in business?

Think about the circumstances / chance meetings / synchronicities / disasters?

What happened? What was the impact?

30) How are you feeling about writing a book?

What excites you? What is getting in the way? What are you choosing to do about it?

31) Are you ready to take action? If not, what is getting in your way? If you are feeling anxious about doing it 'right' remember that no one writes the perfect draft first time. It is called a draft for good reason. The important thing is to get started.

Create a draft plan with timescales for Planning, Writing, Proofreading, Publishing.

It is useful to set up an accountability buddy – share your plan with them and agree how often you'll check in to share progress.

32) Spend some quiet time today thinking about what topic you feel drawn to write about. What is it and why is that important to you?

How will you feel when you see the book on Amazon? How will you use it?

33) Time to start planning – part 1

What is the purpose of your book? To help others? To share your knowledge? To create credibility? To use as a lead generator? To act as a shop window for your goods and services? To leave a legacy? Something else?

Remember you can have multiple reasons but it is helpful to know your purpose before you start.

34) It is useful to know your target audience – I find it easier to write as if I'm talking directly to the target group I've identified

Who are you wanting to help? What is it you want to help them with? How can you help? Men/ women/ both, age profile, social situation, personal/professional

35) Time to choose your first focus. Remember you can write multiple books so there's plenty of scope. Think about what you want your reader to have learned, understand, be able to do etc. by the time they have finished the book. Be as detailed as possible as, when you have clarity, writing the book becomes so much easier.

36) You now know where you are heading, you have your destination. Now it is time to think about the major themes which will allow your reader to achieve what you have planned. Remember nothing is cast in stone and won't be until you actually publish.

Keep it high level – just the title of the chapters/sections. I find it helpful to write each one on a Post-it so I can manipulate, shift and experiment. Doing so allows me to feel free to play with different structures. Remember you can change this as you go along, it is just a starting point. Jot your finished structure outline here.

37) Take each of your chapter/section headings. Now break each one down – identify for each section the major points you want to cover in that section or chapter. Again, keep it brief – at this point you are creating the skeleton of the book. Note your structure here once you have a working structure

38) Now it is time to start writing. Many people put off getting started with writing a book as they think they need a big window of time and it feels overwhelming. It doesn't have to be that way. By breaking the structure into small sections, you can achieve something useful in a small window of time. I find it helpful to make regular appointments with myself in the diary for writing time. Because I break things down into bite size chunks, I can achieve something useful in an hour.

You can choose to write your book sequentially from start to finish or you can choose sections randomly according to your mood or the amount of time you have available.

How are you feeling about getting started on your writing?

39) From now on use this Intentional Journal to:

- Track your progress
- Identify your wins
- Explore anything which is holding you back

What is getting in the way of your writing?

Is this a one off or is there a pattern?

If a pattern is getting in the way think about what is at the root of the issue.

If you want some help, please reach out.

40) Progress to date – How are you going? How are you feeling? Next step?

41) Progress to date – How are you going? How are you feeling? Next step?

42) Progress to date – How are you going? How are you feeling? Next step?

43)   Think about the image you would like to have on the front. Go mining for images. There are lots of sources of inexpensive images. Simply google it...

Think of the key search words and note them here. Create a list of potentials to choose from. Remember to save the link – it is possible to waste lots of time trying to find an image you have seen and liked but cannot find!

44) Progress to date – How are you going? How are you feeling? Next step?

45)   Progress to date – How are you going? How are you feeling? Next step?

46) Progress to date – How are you going? How are you feeling? Next step?

47) You will need a blurb on the cover telling prospective readers what to expect. What are the most important points to include?

Have a look at a few books to give you ideas. Draft your blurb here:

48) Progress to date – How are you going? How are you feeling? Next step?

49) Progress to date – How are you going? How are you feeling? Next step?

50) You will need an "About the Author' Section. What should people know about you? How are you feeling about writing about yourself? If you are finding it difficult ask 3-5 people you trust what they would say about you if they only had 100 words. Then use their words to help you craft your Bio.

Draft it here:

51) Imagine your book is now on Amazon – how does it feel? How are you going to let others know about your book? Time to plan how you will get the word out, so people know it is there to help them.

MY BOOK - MY BUSINESS - MY PROFITS

Think about what it is you want your book to achieve. Be aware that your book can add to your profitability and your success at so many levels. If you plan strategically your books take on a whole different potential. BE INTENTIONAL and the book can become an open door to so many other opportunities.

Think about how your book could be the conduit to other products and services

See my examples below

Book	Products and Services
"Thriving Not Surviving – The 5 Secret Pathways To Happiness Success And Fulfilment"	Free digital copy – lead generator Thriving Not Surviving Journal Thriving Not Surviving – on line Personal and Spiritual Development Programme (Evergreen product) Thrive Together Tribe Membership Group Accelerated – 'Its All About You' coaching programme VIP Intensive days / weekend 'Leadership For Life' Radio Show 'Leadership For Life Media Tour'
Journey Into The New Era Of Profitable	Enlightened Leadership –

Enlightened Leadership	Accelerated 1:1 Programme

Expanded on line accredited Programme

Mastermind groups

Enlightened Leadership Seminars |
| Genuinely New –

Discovering Your New Leadership Identity, Powerful Purpose and Thriving Life After 60. | Media Tour

Email / Consulting Programme

Seminars

VIP Intensive days / weekend |

Further Notes

Record your reflections and the insights you have gained from reading this book:

Further Notes

Record your reflections and the insights you have gained from reading this book:

Further Notes

Record your reflections and the insights you have gained from reading this book:

Further Notes

Record your reflections and the insights you have gained from reading this book:

Further Notes

Record your reflections and the insights you have gained from reading this book:

Further Notes

Record your reflections and the insights you have gained from reading this book:

Further Notes

Record your reflections and the insights you have gained from reading this book:

Further Notes

Record your reflections and the insights you have gained from reading this book:

Further Notes

Record your reflections and the insights you have gained from reading this book:

Further Notes

Record your reflections and the insights you have gained from reading this book:

(I would greatly appreciate it if you also left a review online with your preferred retailer. It would be of enormous help to me and assist other readers find my books and decide to read them. Thank you.)

OPTIONS FOR SUCCESS

If you would like some help there are a number of options open to you:

OPTION 1

VIP INTENSIVES - 1 Day

Here is a personal invitation to join me for an 'Unlock Your Limitless Potential VIP Intensive' where you will start to learn how to unlock the vault of your limitless potential as an Author. The VIP Day is a 4-4 1/2-hour virtual experience (with breaks) starting at $997*

I am able to draw upon my 30 years' experience of helping clients successfully develop confidence and begin to unlock their true potential. In this VIP Day experience, we will create the agenda together to suit where you are now and where you want to be. Potential themes include:

- Identifying the key to unlock your true potential as an Author
- Understanding the patterns which are holding you back
- Creating greater self-worth
- The power of forgiveness – giving yourself the gift
- Creating a strategic way forward

OPTION 2

BECOME THE LEADER OF YOUR OWN LIFE

The VIP INTENSIVE - 2 Day

2x 4-4 1/2-hour virtual experience (with breaks) starting at $1997

I am able to draw upon my 30 years' experience of helping clients to successfully unlock their personal and professional potential. The sessions are engaging and energetically focused. They are designed to help you expand your thinking, to explore how you can step into your genuine power and become the Enlightened Leader of your life.

I recognise your time is precious, so the VIP 2 Day Intensive is customised to suit your specific needs.

A Few Core Themes May Include:

- Understanding your Enlightened Why? (creating and sharing your expanded vision)
- The Power of Mindful Thinking & Greater Self Awareness
- Dealing with Self Limiting Beliefs & Tapping into The Limitless You
- Taking Radical Responsibility for Your Shifts & Empowering Others to Do the Same
- Unlocking Your Hidden Treasures to Elevate Yourself & Your Clients
- Discovering the Power of Communication That Works
- Making the Most Of Your Resources (Time, Energy, Money)
- Creating A Living Legacy

Are you ready to unlock the door to the limitless opportunities which await? Or will you be one of those people who stay stuck in a loop of unawareness of your greater potential? Locked in old paradigm formats that don't support your leadership evolution?

It is time to discover the combinations to unlock the vault and to release your enlightened leadership potential?

How to Claim Your Place...

Set up a 15-minute VIP experience exploration call by emailing me at gina@genuinely-you.com.

Guaranteed Satisfaction: The 15-minute calls are designed to ensure that we are a good fit for one another. This also allows me plan and prepare the day to meet your needs and expectations, so you get the maximum benefit. (There is a no long-term obligation).

OPTION 3

THE ENLIGHTENED LEADERSHIP - ACCELERATOR PROGRAMME

3 months of intensive 1:1 coaching and facilitation with Gina.

Helping you to have the courage to look within to do the deep self-reflection and become the true leader of your life.

Supporting you in your journey to step into your genuine power and release your limitless potential.

Unlocking your unlimited potential to become a shining beacon which inspires and lights the way for others.

The ACCELERATOR PROGRAMME is designed exclusively for those people who are ready to become the spiritual leaders in the new era of consciousness and who recognise time is of the essence!

Set up an exploration call by emailing me at gina@genuinely-you.com.

OPTION 4

THE ENLIGHTENED LEADERSHIP PROGRAMME

A 10-month holistic, fully supported by Enlightened Leadership Facilitators and group coaching from Gina. The programme is accredited by the UK Continuous Professional Development Standards Office.

There are two defined but interconnecting strands to the programme. One focuses on your personal and spiritual development, the other on developing your capacity to be an Enlightened Leader.

Once you have signed up:

Pre-programme Activities

In the first instance, there is a questionnaire designed to create your baseline and for you to identify areas of development.

The Role of The Enlightened Leadership Facilitators

You will be matched with an Enlightened Leadership Facilitator who will act as your support throughout the programme. The programme is designed to help you dig deep and think about your core beliefs, behaviours, past baggage and your dreams and aspirations so there are likely to be times when things feel challenging. Your Leadership Facilitator is there to support and challenge you. To be your champion and coach. Support from your Leadership Facilitator can be accessed via your 1:1 sessions and by email during the month.

Meetings with Your Leadership Facilitator

Before the formal programme begins you will have a 1:1 session via Zoom or Skype to get to know one another, to go through your questionnaire and to agree your project.

You will then meet each month for a 1:1 session with your

facilitator to discuss progress with the programme and your project, identify any blocks and help you overcome them, to support, challenge and celebrate wins with you.

Long Term Project

An ongoing element of the programme is your long-term project. Ideally the project should focus on something which is part of your day to day role. Something you would like to develop which has a significant element requiring the management of others. The project should be agreed with your Leadership Facilitator during your Pre-Programme session.

The Programme Itself

Each month there will be different themes to support your ongoing development. The personal and spiritual themes and principles are introduced via videos, the leadership themes via PowerPoint Presentations and core reading.

Each Unit has a range of activities based on the learning for that unit, designed to help develop your understanding, confidence, and skill base. Your Leadership Facilitator will go through these in your 1:1 sessions.

CPD Standards Office Accreditation

The CPD Standards Office
CPD PROVIDER: 50146
2020-2021
www.cpdstandards.com

Established in 1996, The CPD Certification Service is the independent CPD accreditation centre working across all sectors, disciplines, and further learning applications. ... Hundreds of thousands recognise our CPD Certified symbol as the qualitative benchmark that, not only reflects but also sets those standards.

Accredited CPD training means the learning activity has reached the required Continuing Professional Development standards and benchmarks. The CPD Certification Service provides recognised independent CPD accreditation compatible with global CPD requirements.

CPD ACROSS THE GLOBE

Outside of the UK, CPD extends across the globe and is undertaken in most countries. The CPD Standards Office accreditation services support all forms of professional development and CPD schemes globally, and has an increasingly international reputation as the strongest currency in professional development.

Global Acceptance of CPD Standards Accreditation

The CPD Standards Office has accredited a range of training providers in over 20 countries, across several continents. Due to the research undertaken by the CPD Standards Research Project with various professional bodies and regulators the accreditation is recognised and respected internationally. Formal CPD Standards certificates are issued and accepted in a multitude of countries and across all professional sectors.

The CPD (CE) hours for the programme are 12 hours per month, 120 hours across the 10-month programme. (Please check with your industry / state if you are outside the UK.)

Set up an exploration call by emailing me at gina@genuinely-you.com.

ABOUT THE AUTHOR

GINA GARDINER PROFITS ENHANCER FOR EMPOWERED & ENLIGHTENED LEADERS
Illuminating the Way for you to Create a More Profitable & Meaningful Mission

Gina works with people who are becoming more aware there is a new way: One which requires the courage to take that first leap to look within and discover the new emerging version of yourself. As your consciousness awakens and you start to explore, discover the powerful resources and limitless potential locked inside you, offering you a journey which feels lighter and more expansive. Where everything feels so much more possible and more profitable, enabling you to become the leader of your own life & light the way for others.

Gina Gardiner is a multiple No1 International Bestselling Author, Motivational Speaker, Empowerment and Relationship Coach and Transformational Leadership Trainer with well over 30 years of experience helping people experience happiness, success and fulfilment. She's the founder of Genuinely You and has created a range of personal and spiritual development programmes and 'The Enlightened Leadership' programme.

Gina has learned to walk twice as an adult. For over 20 years, she ran her award-winning school, for the most part from a wheelchair. The gift of this experience was the development of a unique approach to life and to transformational leadership.

ALSO BY GINA GARDINER

Thriving Not Surviving
The 5 Secret Pathways to Happiness, Success and Fulfilment

Chariots on Fire
The Winning Formula for Happiness & Success

The 7 Day Happiness Challenge: With Bonus 30 Day Journal

How You Can Manage Your Staff More Effectively (and Pave Your Way to Your Next Promotion)

Kick-Start Your Career Practical Ideas and Strategies to Support the Development of Leadership

Genuinely New!: Discovering Your New Leadership Identity, Powerful Purpose and Thriving Life After 60

Journey Into The New Era of Profitable Enlightened Leadership: A strategic planner to help you find, define & align yourself as a Profitable Enlightened Leader

It is Time to Become a Beacon of Light & Hope: How To Become An Illuminating Enlightened Leader & Light The Way In Challenging Times

Harnessing the Power of Being an Empath: A Self-Exploration & Empathic Empowerment Guide for Tapping Into Your Limitless Potential

BY RACHEL DAVIDSON
(Assistant to Gina Gardiner and
International Bestselling Novelist, too)

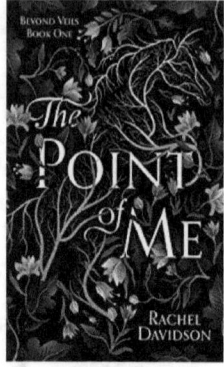 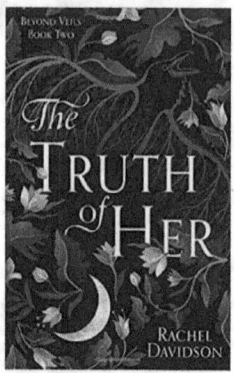 

The Point of Me,
Beyond Veils,
Book One

The Truth of Her,
Beyond Veils,
Book Two

The Hope of Us,
Beyond Veils,
Book Three

Find all these books on Amazon

BY ALINICOLE WATERS
(Mentor to Gina Gardiner)

AliNICOLE WOW! has published several works on Amazon for different industries. You can find her works at www.amazon.com/author/alicianwaters

For a wealth of resources and articles, go to:

https://enlightenedleadership.co

https://genuinely-you.com

https://www.tumblr.com/blog/enlightened-leader-success-vault

And the 'Genuinely You with Gina Gardiner' YouTube Channel

www.ingramcontent.com/pod-product-compliance
Lightning Source LLC
Chambersburg PA
CBHW070417220526
45466CB00004B/1442